SPORTS BRANDS

The Companies at the Center of the Action

By Charlie Beattie

An Imprint of Abdo Publishing
abdobooks.com

abdobooks.com

Published by Abdo Publishing, a division of ABDO, PO Box 398166, Minneapolis, Minnesota 55439.

Printed in the United States of America, North Mankato, Minnesota.
102025
012026

Cover Photo: Isaiah Vazquez/Getty Images Sport/Getty Images
Interior Photos: C. Morgan Engel/NCAA Photos/Getty Images, 1, 23; MI News/NurPhoto/Getty Images, 3, 21; Adam Glanzman/Getty Images Sport/Getty Images, 4–5; Jesse D. Garrabrant/NBAE/National Basketball Association/Getty Images, 6; Tim DeFrisco/Allsport/Getty Images Sport/Getty Images, 7; Nancy Kaszerman/ZUMA Press, Inc./Alamy Live News/Alamy, 9; Chris Graythen/Getty Images Sport/Getty Images, 10; Kelly Kline/WireImage/Getty Images, 11; Tim Warner/Getty Images Sport/Getty Images, 13; Kirby Lee/Kim Hukari/Image of Sport/Alamy, 14–15; Kate Frese/NBAE/National Basketball Association/Getty Images, 16; Alex Trautwig/Major League Baseball/Getty Images, 18; BullDawg2021/Wikimedia Commons, 20; Oleksandr Osipov/Shutterstock Images, 24–25; Joseph Weiser/Icon Sportswire/Getty Images, 26; National Baseball Hall of Fame Library/Major League Baseball/Getty Images, 28; Mark Cunningham/MLB Photos/Getty Images Sport/Getty Images, 30; RF Pictures/The Image Bank/Getty Images, 31; Shutterstock Images, 32; Manan Vatsyayana/AFP/Getty Images, 34–35; Matthias Schrader/AP Images, 36, 45; Simon M. Bruty/Anychance/Getty Images Sport/Getty Images, 38, 47; AP Images, 40; Eliot J. Schechter/National Hockey League/Getty Images, 42; Hubert Fanthomme/Paris Match Archive/Getty Images, 43

Editor: Christa Kelly
Series Designer: Maggie Villaume

Library of Congress Control Number: 2025939204

Publisher's Cataloging-in-Publication Data

Names: Beattie, Charlie, author.
Title: Sports brands: the companies at the center of the action / by Charlie Beattie
Description: Minneapolis, Minnesota: Abdo Publishing, 2026 | Series: The business of sports | Includes online resources and index.
Identifiers: ISBN 9781098298289 (lib. bdg.) | ISBN 9798384932086 (ebook)
Subjects: LCSH: Sports--Juvenile literature. | Sports franchises--Juvenile literature. | Sports personnel--Juvenile literature. | Sport clothes industry--Juvenile literature. | Brands (Commerce)--Juvenile literature. | Sports in popular culture--Juvenile literature.
Classification: DDC 659.144--dc23

TABLE OF CONTENTS

chime
DALLAS
17
WALTON
VISTA
PRINT

CHAPTER ONE

JUMPMAN AND JORDAN BRAND

Luka Dončić of the Dallas Mavericks dribbled slowly as he stared down Jayson Tatum of the Boston Celtics. Just over six minutes remained in the first quarter of Game 1 in the 2024 National Basketball Association (NBA) Finals. A Dallas teammate moved in to set a screen to create space for Dončić to get past his defender. Dončić went around Tatum and then around another defender on his way to the basket. When he got to the rim, three Celtics closed in.

As Tatum and two other Celtics swatted at the ball, Dončić double-clutched his shot. His shoes squeaked on the floor as he hoisted the ball toward the basket. As he fell onto his back, the ball swished through the net.

Luka Dončić, *left*, played for the Dallas Mavericks from 2018 to 2025.

The Boston Celtics beat the Dallas Mavericks 4–1 in the 2024 NBA Finals.

Dončić and Tatum both entered the game hoping for their first NBA championship. But that wasn't the only thing they had in common. Both were also wearing some of the NBA's most popular shoes. Dončić and Tatum were among the many NBA players who swore by Jordan Brand sneakers. The iconic shoes were named after an even more iconic player. And everyone wanted a pair.

The Beginning

In the fall of 1984, every company that made basketball shoes was racing to sign Michael Jordan. The NBA rookie-to-be had been drafted that spring by the Chicago Bulls. Over the summer he had led the United States to the gold medal at the 1984 Olympic Games in Los Angeles. Now everyone wanted to see what the hotshot shooting guard could do in the NBA.

By then, shoe companies were regularly paying the league's top stars to wear the brands' shoes during games. The companies thought that if fans saw a star basketball player running down the court in a company's shiny new shoes, the fans would be more likely to buy the same shoes to wear themselves.

At the time, Converse and Adidas dominated the basketball shoe market. Nike, which made mainly running shoes during its early years, wasn't very involved in the basketball market. But the

Michael Jordan played for the Chicago Bulls for 13 seasons.

BANNED SHOES

In 1985, the NBA had a rule that any shoe worn in a game had to be at least 51 percent white. The first Air Jordans were mostly red and black. Jordan was fined $5,000 by the league each time he wore them. In a shrewd marketing move, Nike agreed to pay each of Jordan's fines. The company played up the fact that the shoe was banned by the league in advertising campaigns. The outlaw angle helped Nike sell 50,000 pairs of the Air Jordan 1.

NBA was growing in popularity, and Jordan was one of the sport's newest stars. Nike saw an opportunity. The company took its entire basketball budget and offered it to Jordan. Jordan decided to take a chance on the company. On October 26, 1984, Jordan signed a $2.5 million shoe deal with Nike. That night, he scored 16 points in his NBA debut.

Nike's gamble soon paid off. Jordan averaged 28.2 points per game in his first season. He won the NBA's Rookie of the Year Award. Nike had the hottest young basketball player on the planet. Now it was time to design a signature shoe for him.

The company created what would become the first Air Jordans. Now simply known as the Jordan 1, the shoes were red, black, and white, matching the Bulls' team colors. To market the shoe, Jordan was photographed in front of the Chicago skyline. The photo was simple. Jordan held a ball in his left hand as he faced a basket. He then jumped up and spread his legs while stretching toward the hoop. It looked like the young star was soaring for a dunk. The famous advertisement

In 2022, an autographed pair of Jordan's game-worn Jordan 1 shoes sold for $120,000.

helped make the Jordan 1 a huge hit when the shoes were released on April 1, 1985.

Becoming a Logo

Each year, Nike created new Air Jordans. When the Air Jordan 3 came out in 1987, the now-famous image from Jordan's first photoshoot was turned into a logo by the shoe's designer,

Tinker Hatfield. The silhouette appeared on the tongue of each shoe and eventually became known as the Jumpman logo.

As the years passed, Jordan became the best player in the NBA. He led the Bulls to six championships in eight years between 1991 and 1998. As the star rose, so did the demand for his shoes.

In 1997, Nike decided to give the superstar his own Nike line. The company named it Jordan Brand. The Jumpman silhouette became the logo.

Though Jordan retired from the NBA for good in 2003, his legacy lives on through Jordan Brand and the Jumpman logo. In 2023, Nike was the most popular shoe brand in the NBA. More than 67 percent of the league's players wore Nikes. Another 7 percent wore Jordan Brand shoes. That made Jordan Brand shoes the third most popular shoes in the league. Many of the players wearing Jordans were the league's top stars, such as Dončić, Tatum, and point guard Chris Paul.

Chris Paul partnered with Jordan Brand in 2008 to release his own Jordan Brand shoes.

Jordan has earned more than $1 billion from his partnership with Nike.

With basketball fans and sneaker collectors buying each new pair of shoes, Jordan Brand has become one of Nike's most profitable divisions. In 2024, Jordan Brand made up roughly 14 percent of Nike's $50 billion in sales. The partnership between Michael Jordan and Nike reached its 40th anniversary in 2024. And though Jordan hasn't played an NBA game in more than two decades, he is still a huge part of the league he helped grow.

Jordans and Beyond

Each year, Nike releases a new version of Air Jordans. For years, fans eager to get their hands on the newest designs have lined up outside shoe stores to buy a pair. The lines became so long that many stores introduced raffles. Instead of lining up, so-called sneakerheads can win the opportunity to buy a pair of the new shoes. Many basketball fans buy shoes because they see their sports idols wearing them. Budding basketball players buy Air Jordans hoping they will improve their own skills.

Since Michael Jordan's historic deal, athlete sneaker deals have become even more common. This has elevated the names of several brands. Golden State Warriors guard Steph Curry signed with Under Armour in 2013. In 2020, the company introduced Curry Brand, Curry's own line.

Shoe deals aren't limited to basketball. During Usain Bolt's reign as the world's fastest sprinter, he had a multimillion-dollar shoe deal with Puma. And superstar quarterback Patrick Mahomes signed with Adidas in 2017.

Whether on or off the court, shoes have long been one way that sports brands align themselves with athletes. But sports brands go far beyond footwear. Companies are constantly thinking up new ways to break into the sports world.

Steph Curry's 2013 deal with Under Armour was worth $4 million per year.

16
Rakuten
GOLDEN
30
STATE

NEW
YOR

CHAPTER TWO

UNIFORMS

Few things in sports are as recognizable as a team's uniform. Some professional sports teams, such as the New York Yankees, Boston Celtics, and Dallas Cowboys, are known all over the world for their jerseys and logos. Each year, millions of jerseys are sold to fans around the globe.

In recent years, jerseys have changed a lot. Teams used to have one home and one road design each season. Now, teams often have a variety of different uniform options to choose from. Unique uniforms have been created for special holidays and promotions. Fans are eager to wear the same jerseys as their sports heroes. Some sports fans are also jersey collectors. The jersey industry has become a big business for sports brands.

Companies often pay professional teams or leagues for the right to be their official

The jersey market is a multibillion-dollar business.

In 2024, Nike signed a deal with the NBA and WNBA to extend their contract until 2037.

uniform suppliers. The NBA is one of the most popular sports leagues in the United States. And each of the league's jerseys carries a Nike logo. The company has held the exclusive rights to the NBA and Women's National Basketball Association (WNBA) uniforms since 2017. With its logo visible on every uniform during every game, Nike receives advertising each time a fan tunes in to an NBA or WNBA game.

Big Names and Big Brands

Several companies battle over the jersey market in the United States. Adidas outfits every Major League Soccer (MLS) team. The company also made uniforms for the National Hockey League (NHL) from 2017 to 2024. A company called Fanatics took over for the 2025 season. However, Nike dominates the majority of the jersey market.

In addition to its NBA and WNBA contracts, Nike supplies every official uniform for the National Football League (NFL). Nike took over that contract after outbidding Reebok in 2012. In 2024, the NFL extended its deal with Nike. Nike is set to make NFL uniforms through the 2038 season.

Nike also took over the manufacturing of Major League Baseball (MLB) uniforms in 2020. Becoming the league's uniform supplier was a big opportunity. For roughly a century, MLB teams worked with companies of their choice to make uniforms. That changed in 1987 when Rawlings became the league's official uniform supplier. The partnership ended in 1991. Later deals with other companies didn't last long either.

A baseball-focused company called Majestic had been licensing MLB clothes since the early 1980s. In 2005, Majestic took over as the league's official uniform supplier. For the next 14 seasons, Majestic made every MLB uniform at its factory in Easton, Pennsylvania.

Each year, more than 1 million jerseys are made at the Easton, Pennsylvania, factory.

In 2019, MLB ended its partnership with Majestic. The league signed a deal with Nike to become MLB's official uniform supplier. Nike partnered with Fanatics to make the uniforms. However, other than the addition of Nike's logo, very little changed about the uniforms. They were even made in the same place. This is because Fanatics had bought Majestic that year. MLB uniforms continued to be produced at the Easton factory.

A Big Blunder

Companies that put their names on sports uniforms gain huge visibility. But that can also lead to embarrassment if something goes wrong. In 2024, Nike and Fanatics debuted new MLB uniforms. The Nike Vapor Premier uniforms were supposed to be lighter and stretchier than previous models. This was supposed to make the uniforms more comfortable for players on hot summer days.

Before teams even left spring training, players were complaining that the uniforms looked and felt cheap. When one player from the San Francisco Giants modeled his team's new uniform, some fans thought they could see through his pants. Another player said the uniforms looked like replicas. That was a big insult. Official jerseys are made from the same material players wear on the field. They often sell for more than $400. Replica jerseys are made for fans to wear casually. They sell for much less.

OUTFITTING THE OLYMPICS

Every four years, countries roll out new clothing and uniform designs for their athletes to wear during the Olympic Games. Many of these designs are made by companies based in those countries. Nike has long outfitted American athletes at the Olympics. Le Coq Sportif is a famous French company. It made French Olympic uniforms from 1912 to 1972. The company won the contract again in 2021 ahead of the 2024 Olympics in Paris, France.

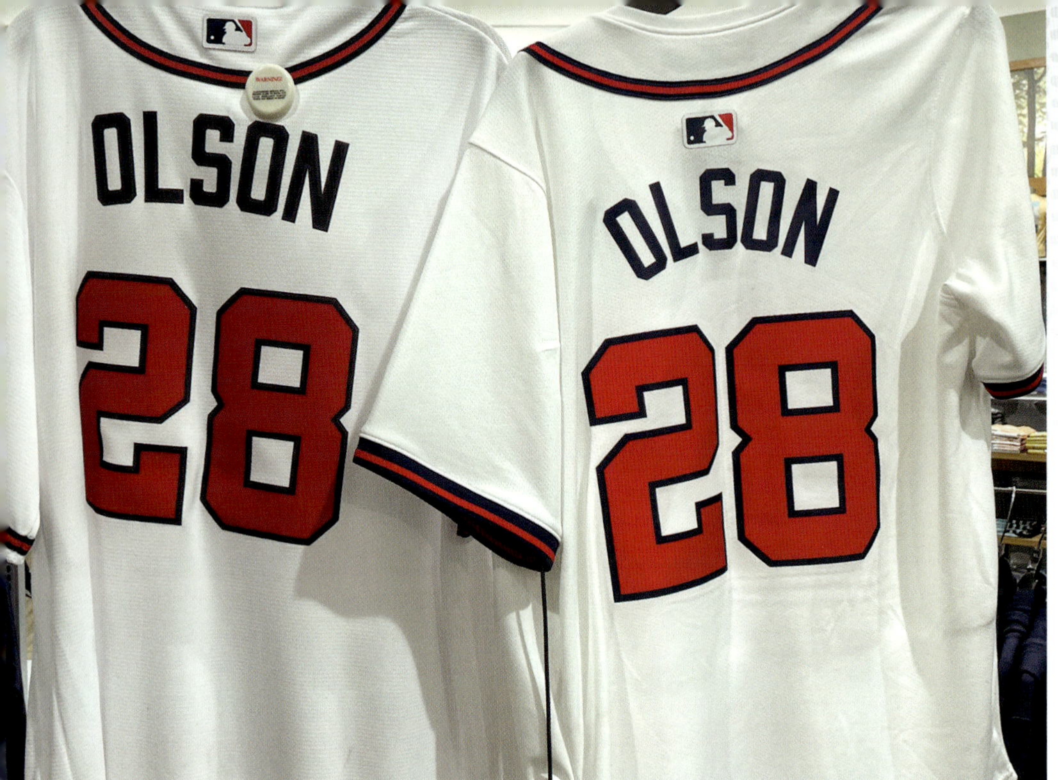

Players and fans complained that the Nike Vapor Premier jerseys, *right*, were uncomfortable and poorly made compared to past MLB jerseys, *left*. One complaint was that the lettering on the new jerseys was too small.

Nike and Fanatics spent the 2024 season reworking the uniforms. They hoped to improve the jerseys before the 2025 season. But that meant the companies had to spend the 2024 season defending their unpopular uniforms. It was a bad look for both Nike and Fanatics. It showed how risky it can be to make products in the sports world.

World Soccer

While many US sports leagues have official uniform suppliers, this is unusual in the world of soccer. MLS is one of the few

In 2019, Puma began manufacturing jerseys for Manchester City. The company gets to display its logo on the team's jerseys.

soccer leagues that supplies uniforms for all of its teams. In most countries, each club works with a company of its choice to create uniforms.

Manufacturing jerseys for one of the world's top soccer teams is a big deal for jersey suppliers. Soccer is the world's most popular sport. And clubs such as Real Madrid in Spain, Italy's Juventus, and England's Manchester United have fans around the globe. Partnerships with these teams can give big boosts to the suppliers' sales.

Another reason soccer clubs are such big prizes for jersey suppliers is that soccer uniforms change frequently. US sports teams often keep the same designs for several seasons, and some keep the same designs for decades. But many soccer clubs change their designs each year. The new uniforms are often rolled out with big promotional photoshoots or fashion shows. Fans excitedly await these reveals. If they like the designs, some will buy authentic or replica versions of the jerseys. Popular designs can make jersey suppliers huge profits.

College Uniforms

In 2021, a landmark decision gave US college athletes the ability to profit off their names, images, and likenesses (NIL). That meant college players could appear in commercials and accept sponsorship deals. Before the ruling, accepting NIL deals would have made players ineligible to play college sports.

Under the old rules, jersey suppliers could make a replica uniform featuring a college star's number. But the player's name could not appear on it. Players were also banned from making money from jersey sales.

Connecticut basketball star Paige Bueckers was one of the first athletes to benefit from the new NIL rules. She quickly

Paige Bueckers made an estimated $1.4 million from NIL deals during her last college season in 2024–25.

became one of college basketball's most marketable stars. This was good news for Nike. The company made Connecticut's basketball uniforms.

Nike sold copies of Buecker's No. 5 jersey. The jersey became one of college basketball's biggest sellers. As the star point guard led the Huskies to the 2025 national title, her white home and blue road jerseys were the top two selling women's college basketball jerseys in the country.

Wilson
INDOOR GAME BALL
EVO NXT

CHAPTER THREE

SPORTS EQUIPMENT

In 2022, millions of fans tuned in to the first round of the National Collegiate Athletic Association (NCAA) men's and women's basketball tournaments. As the games started, viewers noticed something different about the basketballs on the court. Each ball was a bright shade of orange. Most game-used basketballs are shades of darker orange or brown. Fans had not seen an NCAA basketball so bright before. Immediately, the ball became a hot topic.

A company called Wilson had made the ball. The company had been supplying the official balls for the NCAA Tournaments since 2002. The new basketball model was called the Evo NXT. The new ball brought out strong reactions from fans. Many said it was distracting. Billionaire Mark Cuban, who owned the NBA's Dallas Mavericks at

Wilson designed the Evo NXT to be a bright shade of orange to help players see it across the court.

The Evo NXT is designed to allow players to shoot from farther distances.

the time, said it looked "like a $5.99 ball." Wilson took to social media to assure Cuban that the ball was not cheap.

Players weren't sure about the new ball either. None of the tournament participants had used the Evo NXT before.

While Wilson makes the balls for the NCAA Tournaments, each school chooses its own brand of ball during the regular season. Some players thought the new ball was hard to shoot with. Others said it bounced strangely off the floor and the glass.

Despite the initial reaction, the Evo NXT survived. The bright orange ball appeared in the NCAA Tournaments for a fourth time in 2025. However, the backlash highlighted the risks of innovation in a sports brand. Companies such as Wilson are always looking to make positive changes to their equipment, but sometimes people have bad reactions to new products. That can bring negative attention to a company.

Bat Battles

Sports equipment is constantly changing. Brands put years of study into the science of sports gear in hopes of creating the best products for top-level players. These new products then help brands get noticed. When fans see their sports heroes using new equipment, they rush to stores to get their own.

One of the earliest examples of a brand partnering with a major athlete took place more than a century ago. According to the legend, a 17-year-old named Bud Hillerich from Louisville, Kentucky, convinced local baseball star Pete Browning to try his homemade bat in 1884. Browning was a player for the Louisville Eclipse of the American Association, a professional

Bud Hillerich originally made each bat by hand.

league at the time. When Browning had success with the new bat, Hillerich and his father were flooded with orders from other players.

The story is likely false. But Hillerich and his father did create the Hillerich & Bradsby company. The company still makes its famous Louisville Slugger bats. It is one of the most recognizable baseball brands in the world.

For more than a century, Louisville Slugger bats were the most popular bats in MLB. They were made from the wood of ash trees, a wood chosen because it was both lightweight and strong. But in the late 1990s, players began questioning whether ash was the best wood for bats. A Canadian man named Sam Holman created a maple bat. MLB approved it for use in games. It became known as the SAM bat. When legendary slugger Barry Bonds used a maple bat to set the MLB home run record in 2001, maple bats became the go-to style.

Brands raced to produce their own bats. One of the most successful brands was Marucci. Jack Marucci founded the Louisiana company in 2002. He was an athletic trainer at Louisiana State University, which had produced several MLB players. He worked with them to grow the company.

Within two decades, Marucci was one of the top bat makers in the world. The company tailored the bats to players' needs. Consumers loved this. By 2016, 40 percent of MLB players were using Marucci bats. The next year, the company bought out one of its top competitors, Victus Sports. Marucci continued making bats under both names.

In 2025, Marucci and Victus became the official bats of MLB. Players were still free to use whichever brand they liked, but

Marucci designs custom bats for MLB players by examining its clients' balance, strength, and swing.

Marucci and Victus bats were marketed by the league. It was a stunning rise for a company that took an innovative approach to equipment.

The Perfect Helmet

A lot of sports equipment is designed with safety in mind. There's no better example of this than the evolution of football helmets. In football's early days, players wore leather helmets without face masks. Plastic helmets first debuted in the 1950s. For the next five decades, the padding inside helmets grew thicker, but helmet designs didn't change much. They were smooth domes, and they offered the same protection to all players.

Leather football helmets were common by the 1920s but offered limited protection.

During the 2000s, the NFL saw a spike in concussions. This caused many parents to steer their kids away from playing football. The NFL poured millions of dollars into research on safer helmets. Many sports brands joined the race to make safer equipment.

Helmet makers such as Riddell, Schutt, and VICIS started creating new designs. They ditched the smooth domes and started making helmets that matched the shape of the human head. Soon, NFL players took to the field in many unique designs that featured strategic indents on the tops, sides, and backs of helmets.

In the 2020s, companies went even further and started designing NFL helmets for specific positions. Since linemen slam into each other on each play, VICIS designed the trench helmet with more front and side padding. Research showed

THE GUARDIAN CAP

In 2024, the NFL began allowing another layer of protection on top of football helmets. Guardian Caps are soft coverings worn over football helmets to help prevent concussions. Guardian Sports, a Georgia-based company, designed the first Guardian Cap in 2012. Players have worn them during practice since 2022. The NFL approved them for use in games two years later.

that most quarterbacks suffered head injuries when they hit the ground after sacks. VICIS developed a helmet that protects quarterbacks in these situations.

While the average fan doesn't buy these helmets, making them is still a top priority for companies. The football world is constantly looking to make the game safer. And creating safer helmets can lead to deals with youth football organizations and high schools all over the United States. Creating safer equipment can lead to big profits.

Rawlings makes more than 2 million baseballs each year.

CASE STUDY

SPALDING VERSUS RAWLINGS

Approximately 120 baseballs are used in every MLB game. Over the course of the league's 2,430 regular-season games each year, that adds up to about 291,000 baseballs per season. Every one of those baseballs is made by Rawlings.

Rawlings is one of the most recognizable baseball brands in the world. In addition to supplying baseballs for MLB, the company makes bats, gloves, and other equipment. Rawlings even supplied MLB uniforms for many years.

Until the 1970s, MLB baseballs were made by Spalding. One of Spalding's biggest breakthroughs was the standardized baseball in 1876. Prior to that, players made their own balls.

By 1955, Spalding was the second-largest sporting equipment company in the country. Rawlings was close behind in fourth. Spalding hired Rawlings to make MLB balls with the Spalding name on them. This arrangement continued for more than 20 years.

Spalding's contract with MLB was up for renewal in 1976. When Spalding quoted the league a hefty price to keep making baseballs, the league decided to end its partnership with Spalding. But instead of finding a new supplier, MLB partnered directly with Rawlings. Beginning in the 1977 season, Rawlings became MLB's official baseball supplier, with its own name on the balls. The company and the league have remained partners ever since.

arena

CHAPTER FOUR

TOOLS OF THE TRADES

At the 2024 Olympic swimming competition in Paris, no event was closer than the men's 200-meter freestyle race. As the competitors came down the last stretch, David Popovici of Romania, Matthew Richards and Duncan Scott of Great Britain, and Luke Hobson of the United States were neck and neck. When the competitors hit the wall, they were so close that announcers weren't immediately sure who had won.

Within seconds, the results popped up. Popovici had won the race. Richards was second, and Hobson third. Scott missed out on a medal. But he was just 0.15 seconds behind the winner.

The tight race highlighted the need for precise timing at the Olympics. And for nearly a century, one company has been making its name as the official timer of Olympic events. The OMEGA

Romania's David Popovici pulled ahead from third place to first place in the final five meters to win the men's 200-meter freestyle race at the 2024 Olympics.

Popovici, *center*, earned Romania its first Olympic gold medal in men's swimming.

watch company of Switzerland stakes its reputation on being accurate. And that helps the company sell hundreds of thousands of watches each year.

OMEGA is just one example of a company that has a specific role in the sports world. These companies take their roles very seriously. Their commitment to excellence translates to both name recognition and big profits.

Keeping the Time

In 1932, OMEGA sent a watchmaker from Switzerland to the Olympics in Los Angeles. He carried with him 30 chronographs.

They were early handheld stopwatches. The pieces were accurate within one-tenth of a second. Since then, OMEGA has been the official timekeeper for the Olympics.

While the company's original stopwatches were impressive, they had flaws. Each stopwatch had to be operated by an individual person. A timekeeper pushing the stopper down a fraction of a second late could cost a competitor a race.

BRAND AMBASSADORS

Athletes who represent companies are often called brand ambassadors. OMEGA hired American swimmer Michael Phelps to promote the brand before the 2008 Olympics in Beijing, China. That decision paid off when Phelps won a record eight gold medals in Beijing in one of the most famous Olympic performances ever.

In 1968, OMEGA introduced touch pads to Olympic pools. Once a racer hit the pad, the watch that timed that competitor stopped. These automatic timing systems were accurate to a thousandth of a second.

The advance in technology arrived just in time. Four years later at the Summer Games in Munich, West Germany, the new system helped break a tie in the men's 400 individual medley. Swede Gunnar Larsson won the event over American Tim McKee after their times were examined. Larsson's time was 4 minutes, 31.981 seconds. McKee finished in 4:31:983.

In 2024, OMEGA timed and scored all 329 Olympic events.

OMEGA continues to fine-tune its timing each year. At track events, high-speed cameras take photographs of the finish. These pictures can be lined up with the clock to determine a winner in tight races.

Traditionally, track athletes pose next to their races' clocks for victory photos. Above the time, a giant OMEGA logo is displayed. This helps advertise the company. The strategy works. In 2023, OMEGA sold more than 570,000 watches. The company made nearly $2.9 billion.

Fueling Up

The University of Florida Gators football team often practices and plays in the state's famously brutal heat. In the mid-1960s, assistant coach Dewayne Douglas was worried that his players might be dehydrated. He spoke to Dr. Robert Cade, who studied kidney function in the university's medical school.

Cade and three colleagues got to work on developing a drink that would help the football team stay healthy in the heat. After discovering that the average player was losing approximately eight quarts (7.6 L) of sweat in two hours, Cade's team knew they needed something that would restore players' electrolytes and carbohydrates.

Cade's team designed a sports drink that came in both orange and lemon-lime flavors. The football players drank it during their practices and found that they were less tired and performed better. When the Gators started winning, everyone wanted to know their secret. That's when the world learned about Gatorade.

Cade and his team eventually sold the rights to the drink to the Stokely-Van Camp food company. Soon it was in stores around the country and well on its way to becoming the sports drink of choice for athletes. By the 1980s, Gatorade was on nearly every major sideline. Players not only drank it but also often used it to celebrate. When the New York Giants

The Stokely-Van Camp company acquired the rights to Gatorade in 1967.

won Super Bowl XXI in January 1987, they dumped a cooler of Gatorade over the head of coach Bill Parcells. This Gatorade bath soon became an iconic sports tradition.

Gatorade didn't stop at in-game hydration. In the 2000s, the company evolved to create additional items such as gels to fuel workouts and recovery drinks to help athletes heal after games and tough practices. Having so many products helped Gatorade dominate the sports-drink market. The company sold more than $7 billion worth of products in 2024.

The Sports-Drink Market

Gatorade's unique backstory and longtime success give it brand recognition. That means many people have heard of the product. When they see it on shelves, they are more likely to buy it because of its familiar name. Gatorade, which is now owned by Pepsi, keeps up that image by partnering with sports leagues. It is the official drink of the NFL, NBA, WNBA, and NASCAR.

Other companies have carved out their own spaces in the drink market. Powerade partners with several sports organizations. These organizations include the International Federation of Association Football (FIFA) and the NCAA.

Over the years, Powerade and Gatorade have been criticized for the amount of sugar in their drinks. The brands responded by making zero-sugar options. But other companies have taken on Gatorade and Powerade by creating what they claim are healthier sports drinks. Bodyarmor was founded in 2011. The company's sports drinks are made with coconut water and natural ingredients to lower both the salt and sugar content.

In 2021, Coca-Cola, which owns Powerade, bought Bodyarmor. In the competitive world of sports drinks, the small company now had huge help in getting its name out. Bodyarmor struck its first major sports deal in 2024. The company partnered with the NHL as its official drink supplier.

Bodyarmor and the NHL signed a deal lasting until 2029.

Bodyarmor took over the contract after a similar brand, BioSteel, went bankrupt.

Sports brands play big roles at all levels of sports. They provide jerseys, tools, and fuel for athletes. In return, brands become well known around the world, leading to big profits. As the world of sports grows, sports brands will find new opportunities to serve athletes and rake in money.

CASE STUDY

TECHNOGYM

Athletes need fitness equipment to help them train. Nerio Alessandri began building fitness equipment in his garage in the early 1980s. He launched Technogym in the 1980s and quickly gained success marketing his products to both at-home consumers and sports leagues. By 1986, Alessandri had struck deals with top Italian soccer team AC Milan. Four years later, Technogym supplied fitness equipment for all 24 nations competing in the 1990 World Cup.

Alessandri didn't stop there. He brought his fitness equipment to the world of Formula One racing. Then he signed deals with top drivers Ayrton Senna and Michael Schumacher.

Technogym continued to branch out into other sports such as tennis, golf, and sailing. But its biggest partnership is with the Olympic Games. Technogym first began supplying equipment to athletes staying in the Olympic Village at the 2000 Games in Sydney, Australia. The 2024 Olympic and Paralympic Games in Paris marked Technogym's ninth Olympics as the official supplier of wellness equipment.

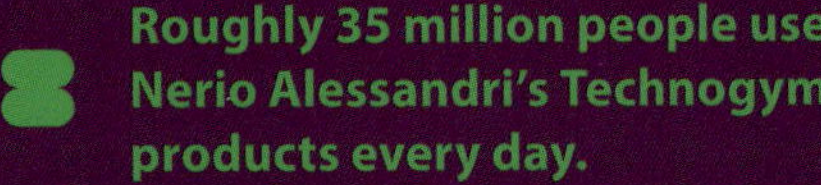

Roughly 35 million people use Nerio Alessandri's Technogym products every day.

TIMELINE

1884

Bud Hillerich makes the first Louisville Slugger bat for professional baseball player Pete Browning.

1960s

Dr. Robert Cade and his colleagues invent Gatorade.

1977

Rawlings takes over for Spalding as the official supplier of MLB's game balls.

1984

On October 26, Michael Jordan signs a $2.5 million shoe deal with Nike.

1997

Nike creates the Jordan Brand, incorporating Jordan's famous Jumpman logo.

2000

Technogym partners with the Olympic Games for the first time.

2005

Majestic becomes the official uniform supplier of MLB.

2019

Nike takes over as the official uniform supplier of MLB.

2022

Wilson debuts the Evo NXT ball at the men's and women's NCAA basketball tournaments.

2024

The NFL approves the Guardian Cap for players to wear over their helmets during games.

2025

Marucci and Victus become the official bats of MLB.

GLOSSARY

ambassador
A person who represents or promotes something.

bankrupt
Unable to pay a debt, often leading to a business closing.

carbohydrate
A nutrient found in food that is broken down and converted to use for energy.

concussion
A brain injury caused by a blow to the head or a violent shaking of the head and body.

dehydrated
Having a condition in which the body does not have enough water.

division
A part or section of something.

electrolyte
A substance that helps a person's body regulate chemical reactions.

iconic
Well known for excellence.

innovation
The process of changing or improving something.

licensing
Paying to use images or brands belonging to another company or person.

retire
To end one's career.

rookie
A professional athlete in their first year of competition.

sponsorship
Money given to an athlete, team, or league in return for supporting a company's products publicly.

supplier
A person or company that provides goods.

MORE INFORMATION

BOOKS

Illustrated Sports Encyclopedia. DK, 2023.

Rowell, Rebecca. *Gatorade: Sports Drink Innovator*. Abdo, 2024.

Rule, Heather. *Athletes as Influencers: Name, Image, and Likeness*. Abdo, 2026.

ONLINE RESOURCES

To learn more about sports brands, please visit **abdobooklinks.com** or scan this QR code. These links are routinely monitored and updated to provide the most current information available.

INDEX

ABOUT THE AUTHOR

Charlie Beattie is a writer, editor, and former sportscaster. Originally from Saint Paul, Minnesota, he now lives in Charleston, South Carolina, with his wife and son.